PROJECT ARCHIVE:

An architectural survey of socially engaging extracanonical works

VOLUME 1: SOCIALLY ENGAGING MODES OF DOMESTICITY

NOVATO, CA

Acknowledgments

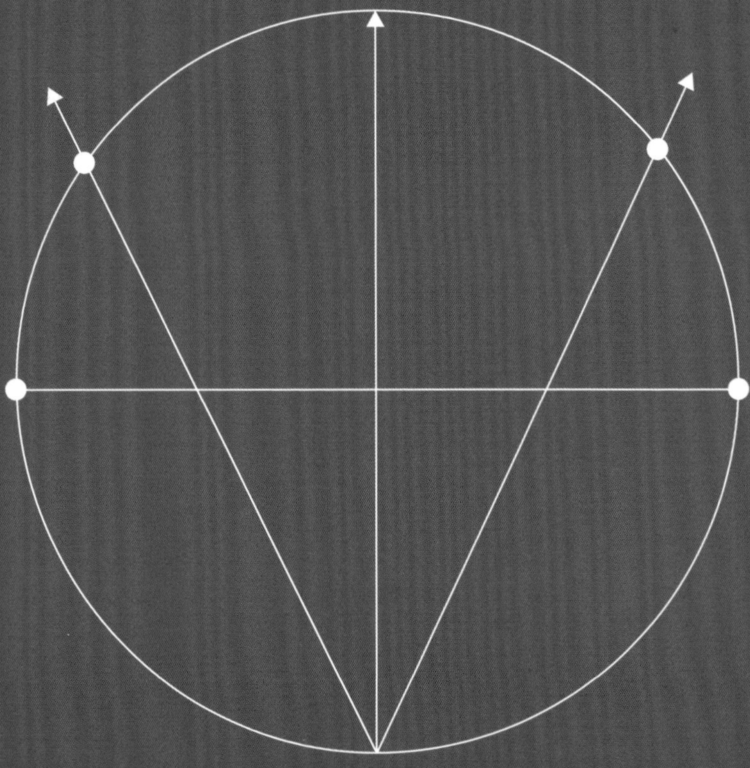

SPECIAL THANKS TO
Amy Kulper
Ijlal Muzzafar

FUNDED BY
Ishum Fund
Choi Fund
Spur Fund
RISD Social Equity and Inclusion
RISD Department of Architecture and Design

ADVISED BY
Soul Brown
Sarah Cunningham
Namita Dharia
Kevin Janakowski
Amy Kulper
Léopold Lambert
Jess Myers
Rebecca Nolan
Christopher Roberts
Mindy Seu
Paul Solelis
Ramon Tejada

CONTRIBUTING WRITERS
Yasmine El Alaoui El Abdallaoui
Ara Anderson
Zaara Arsiwala
Deji Eclarin
Leslie Ponce-Diaz
Derek Russell
Alison Sherpa
Cherry Yang

About

We believe that the current architectural canon is an active agent in perpetuating our current global environmental and humanitarian crises.

This canon, dictated by Western institutions, has promoted a limited understanding of architecture and the social and political inequalities that it underwrites. Thus architecture's role is reduced to only shelter instead of as a political actant in society—i.e. its impact on people and their daily lives is rarely considered. We are invested in seeing architecture as a social project. We advocate for architecture that prioritizes works that go beyond their formal elements. Where both aesthetics and its ability to serve the urgent social needs of a community are equally important.

Thus, we research and collate socially engaging projects that have addressed these ongoing issues in our community.

Architecture publications often forefront the latest sustainable product. The dissemination of these technologies often disregards pre-existing regionally specific works. It also ignores socio-cultural traditions entangled with architecture. Utilizing extra-canonical works, can provide insight into value systems around the world that puts people and the well-being of their environment first. This promotes socially engaging and sustainable building strategies, as opposed to inaccessible technology-oriented solutions.

We give voice to people who present a diverse range of thought and make their work visible and accessible.

We crowdsourced our content from varied sources to allow for a multi-authored narrative. We have reached out to members at varied levels within academic institutions, architecture enthusiasts, and independent researchers to contribute to the archive. Additionally, we believe that a direct and transparent channel into the perspective of the individuals in the communities are made visible through an audio-recorded interview. Through these recordings on our website, we are able to integrate oral histories into the archive.

We embrace the archive as this generation's method of course correction.

We are invested in the construction of the future of the discipline, as a continuously evolving body of knowledge. The archive to us is an ever-growing collection of projects within the architectural practice preserved as interrelated sets. All works, despite their varied characteristics, are of value.

Preface

Volume 1 closely assesses and challenges the existing model of residential architecture as perpetuated by the Western architectural discipline. The extractionist view on nature developed during the Industrial Revolution not only contributes toward our socio-environmental issues, but continues to invalidate regional sources of knowledge that work in tandem with nature. Communities that held pertinent information on how to build in harmony with the natural environment were instead defined as culturally deficient and technologically challenged.

Hence, we chose to examine "domesticities" as opposed to "residential architecture" to go beyond the cannon's understanding of "housing." Through this lens, we are able to closely examine different "ways of living and designing domestic spaces" at select sites in the Global South. We categorized our findings in four distinct ways.

REFORMING TRADITIONAL MODES OF DOMESTICITY HIGHLIGHTS PROJECTS that have drawn inspiration from both traditional architecture and modernisms of the time.

RESPONSE TO CONDITIONS OF THE LANDSCAPE HIGHLIGHTS PROJECTS that methodologically survey sites and how architecture interacts with it.

RESPONSE TO ENVIRONMENTAL CRISES HIGHLIGHTS PROJECTS that react to urgencies post-natural disasters and evolving climatic conditions. Response to Societal Crises highlights projects that are influenced by socio-political events. These include projects that provide solutions to education access inequities, housing shortages, lack of community building spaces, and more.

Furthermore, in our index we refer to local architects, construction by self-reliant community members, and thoughtful collaboration between architects of varied backgrounds and nationalities. This criteria was made not only for their expertise and knowledge of the area but also to promote and acknowledge the globalized nature of the current architectural discipline.

Expanding one's understanding of domesticity in architecture allows for designers to create works that respond to the immediate needs of the local population and other parallel ecosystems. It advocates for acknowledgment of the agency social, political, and environmental actatants have on the conception and implementation of their work. Most importantly, it gives voice to people in contemporary practice of architecture who were historically dismissed.

Defining Ease of Research

Through researching these projects, we have developed a classification technique that assigns a level of difficulty (easy, medium, hard) to finding each precedent. While a writer's own experience with researching adds to a certain level of subjectivity, this classification shows how visible a project is both in the space of libraries and online research.

EASY

Most information needed to archive a project is available online. There is no need to refer to books or library sources.

Multiple useful search results are available on search engines. There are many sources and the information is diverse. The first page of search engine results is sufficient to document the project.

The information correlates with keywords entered on the search engine.

Company websites can easily be accessed.

Information about the principal architects and founders is available.

Information about a project is also available on popular architecture blogs like *Archdaily* and *Divisare.*

Books by established companies, architecture critics, and writers are available and can be used as a primary source to document a project.

Multiple high-resolution images are available

MEDIUM

Some information is available online but may need to refer to certain library sources like books and academic journals.

There are some useful search results on search engines. There are fewer sources and the information is repetitive. The first three pages of the search engine results are sufficient to document the project.

The information in search results doesn't always correlate with keywords entered in the search engine.

Company websites can't be easily accessed.

Information about principal architects/founders are not easily available, i.e., less or no biography and background of the firm or architect are available.

Information is not easily available on popular architecture blogs like *Archdaily* and *Divisare,* instead, news journals and other architectural blogs/archives are used.

Some sources are available at an academic library with architecture-related information. These might need to be paired with online research to fulfill the format of documentation of the archive.

Few high-quality images are available or images found are often of a lower resolution.

HARD

There is little to no information available online. There is a need to refer to certain library sources like books and academic journals. Often library sources other than your own institutions or public libraries are used.

Results from search engines are sparsely distributed throughout multiple sources. If found, there are few sources and the information is repetitive.

The information doesn't always correlate with keywords entered on the search engines.

Company website can't be easily accessed and if found, is not updated, can't be used because of the researcher's location, or has very little to no description of the project.

The company was established prior to the 1990s; thus, not well documented online.

Information about principal architects/founders is not available.

Information is not easily available on popular architecture blogs like *Archdaily* and *Divisare,* and instead, news journals and other architectural blogs/archives are used. These blogs provide very little architecture-related information about the project.

Very few sources are available at an academic library with very little architecture-related information.

Few to no lower resolution images available.

Table of Contents

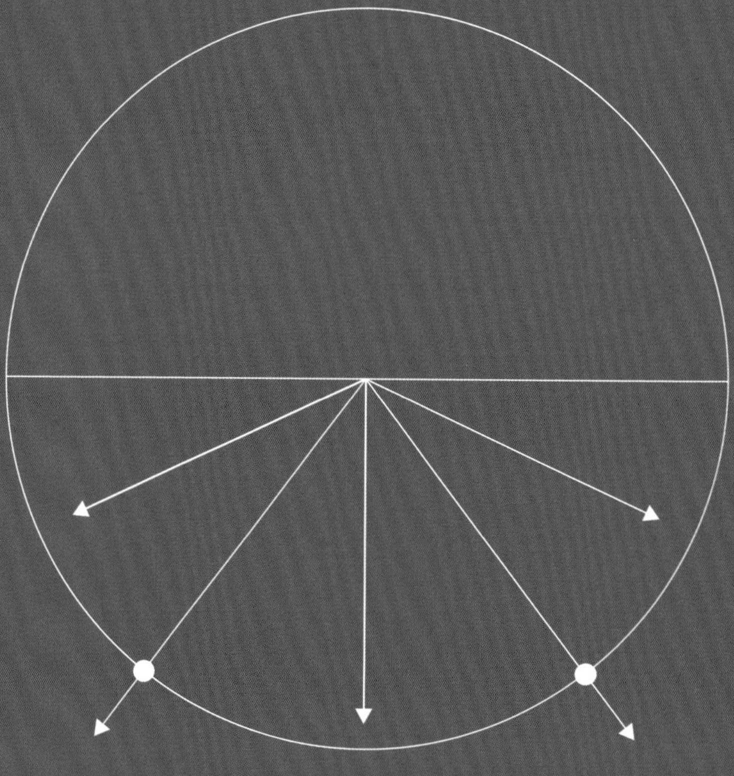

SELECTED PROJECTS

FROM THE ARCHIVE

Ancon Building
Planta

Sliding glass doors and a generously sized balcony creates a seamless indoor-outdoor relationship. The bamboo screen on the façade works both as a shading device and also adds a natural texture to the site's immediate urban environment. This double layered façade consists of a bamboo screen and glass façade. The layered façade allows both residents and pedestrians to have a semi-porous view out of and into the building.[1]

BUENOS AIRES, ARGENTINA

Year completed: 2015 | Level of Difficulty: Easy

Climate: Temperate[2] | Key Attribute: Layered Façade

Casa Cinco Patios
Planta

This project went through extensive remodeling centered around creating outdoor spaces that have alternative uses. The project consists of a side yard that works as an extension of the interior of the house, a back patio, and an entrance courtyard with a fountain and a terrace.

The terrace also can be easily accessed from their studio and contains a green roof with a pergola and a place for barbecues.[3]

BUENOS AIRES, ARGENTINA

Year completed: 2015 | Level of Difficulty: Easy

Climate: Tropical[4] | Key Attribute: Multi-Use Outdoor Spaces

1376

Extension of Identity House
Paseo Architecture

This project is an extension to an existing house that utilizes traditional building methods. New cantilevered stairs connect the extension and the original house, mimicking the previous circulation path. The new stairs utilize modern materials like steel; however, the use of wood cladding on the interior walls of the stairs allude to traditional village homes.[5]

SANTA CRUZ, BOLIVIA

Year completed: 2012 | Level of Difficulty: Medium

Climate: Mediterranean[6] | Key Attribute: Extension

Swahili Gem Apartments
Urko Sanchez Architects

The project features a façade detail that alludes to traditional latticed wood screens known as mashrabiyas. This screen covers three sides of the apartment building, and also functions as a primary structural component for the walls set behind. Balconies and terraces are situated on the fourth side to provide residents with a complete view of the nearby creek. The skin was developed in collaboration with local and international engineers along with steelworkers on site.[7]

MOMBASA, KENYA

Year completed: 2017 | Level of Difficulty: Easy

Climate: Tropical[8] | Key Attribute: Screened Façade

Wind Tower Housing Complex
AGi Architects

SALMIYA, KUWAIT

Year completed: 2019 | Level of Difficulty: Easy

Climate: Desert[10] | Key Attribute: Single-Family Housing Complex

This project is based in a rapidly urbanizing area with multi-generational homes, as well as young adults looking for homes. The high-rise apartment fulfills demand for a modern home with reference to traditional architecture. The programs that used to be conducted in a courtyard space are now conducted at the large terrace. Thus referencing traditional architecture in the setting of a single-family dwelling.[9]

KHALIFA SCHOOL
Gulf English School

Galpon House
2172 / Asociados

This project is located on a site surrounded by pine trees on one side, and Lake Rapel on the other side. Cost-effective and weatherproof materials are utilized to achieve the feeling of a country house that mimics the style of the surrounding farm sheds. Additionally, the use of relatively organic materials like wood on the lower level visually integrates the façade of the project in its landscape.[11]

LAGO RAPEL, CHILE

Year completed: 2019 | Level of Difficulty: Easy

Climate: Temperate[12] | Key Attribute: Lake View

Game Lodge
Slee & Co Architects

The project is a low-slung linear structure set on the red earth of the its site. The red sand from the site is added to the plaster to blend the linear structure into the vast red landscape of the hunting farm. Furthermore, the weight of the roof rests on a diagonal supporting wall of the building to reduce the support column on the exterior. This prevents any obstructions while viewing the landscape.[13]

UNKNOWN, NAMIBIA

Year completed: 2018 | Level of Difficulty: Easy

Climate:Arid[14] | Key Attribute: Red Earth Façade

Topo House
Martín Dulanto Arquitecto

This project consists of A public entry-level floor that is submerged in the ground, hidden in plain sight. This allows the project to appear smaller than the area it occupies. The top floors hover over this excavated volume and contain private living spaces. The bedroom windows are oriented toward the mountain range, and lagoon and away from the public front yard.[15]

LIMA, PERU

Year completed: 2018 | Level of Difficulty: Easy

Climate: Desert[16] | Key Attribute: Hill House

Tropical Box House
WHBC Architects

Situated in the jungle, the project embraces the canopy. This house is made up of a gridded concrete façade that allows for plant growth over time. A double façade also safeguards from the tropical sun and rain, while also allowing for light to filter in. The house is also built on stilts to level the floor with the canopy, which keeps pests out of the dwelling and lowers humidity.[17]

KUALA LUMPUR, MALAYSIA

Year completed: 2012 | Level of Difficulty: Easy

Climate: Tropical[18] | Key Attribute: Porous Façade

Villa Saxo
Studio Saxe

This project is a family home that combines modern methods of construction with local materials and techniques. Villa Saxo is defined by an exoskeleton pergola structure that provides shade over large terraced areas. It also creates a frame for the local flora to grow around, which will eventually envelope the house with plants.[19]

GUANACASTE, COSTA RICA

Year completed: 2017 | Level of Difficulty: Medium

Climate: Tropical [20] | Key Attribute: Building Envelope

House in the Páramo
NLE architects

This project sits in the Andean Moorelands, a cloud forest with a fragile ecosystem. The soil in this ecosystem is extremely sensitive to major changes. To reduce impacting underground water flows, the structure is elevated with concrete pillars designed to work without a floor beam holding them together. Additionally, the house uses prefabricated pieces so that assembly can be done by hand, and no machinery is required on site.[21]

PÁRAMO, COLOMBIA

Year completed: 2021 | Level of Difficulty: Easy

Climate: Tropical[22] | Key Attribute: Elevated Structure

Bioclimatic Prototype of a Host and Nectar Garden Building
NLE architects

CALI, COLOMBIA

Year completed: 2012 | Level of Difficulty: Medium

Climate: Tropical[24] | Key Attribute: Nectar Garden

The region faced a significant loss of forest land and biodiversity. As butterflies can be used as a biometer to gauge diversity within an ecosystem, this project is a model for domestic spaces that help to increase the butterfly population. The backyard consists of green walls with native plants, and are maintained by the textile collective that lives and works in the space. The workers ship the seeds from the garden to neighboring communities to cumulatively create a "green corridor" in the area for the butterfly populations to migrate between yards.[23]

Plan B Guatemala
DEOC Arquitectos

Plan B Guatemala was created for displaced families in response to the Volcán de Fuego eruption in June 2018. The construction makes use of long-lasting building materials that are easy to find and to work with, such as cinder blocks, bamboo, and steel plate roofing. Cinder Blocks are used expressively in different dispositions, creating a permeable lattice that protects the inner areas from the outside, allowing for natural ventilation throughout the spaces. Even though this is a replicable housing model, the pop of color inside the cinder block holes allows for members to add a customizable detail to their home.[25]

EL PAREDÓN BUENA VISTA, GUATEMALA

Year completed: 2018 | Level of Difficulty: Medium

Climate: Tropical[26] | Key Attribute: Cinder Block

SOS Children's Village
Urko Sanchez Architects

TADJOURAH, DJIBOUTI

Year completed: 2014 | Level of Difficulty: Easy

Climate: Desert[28] | Key Attribute: Medina

The medina (a walled city containing narrow and maze like streets) that this project exists in has no cars on the streets to create space for children to roam, as well as open spaces and lots of vegetation for the residents to care for their plants. It consists of 15 houses that run family strengthening programs. These houses have similar layouts and are arranged in a manner that provides shade to one another and creates meandering alleyways.[27]

1

NONLA 4eme MONDA

OTHER PROJECTS FROM THE ARCHIVE

ALMA-EL CHAAB, LEBANON

Year completed: 2003 | Level of Difficulty: Medium

Climate: Mediterranean[30] | Key Attribute: Reconfigured Plan

Alma-El Shaab

Almimariya Architects and Designers for Sustainable Development

The firm works on architecture that is responsive to its context. This particular project draws inspiration from traditional Lebanese architecture and has a stone façade with a red-tiled roof. To adapt the residence to the humid summers of its site, the structural layout is changed from a square to an "H" in plan, which provides different views of the landscape and allows a cool breeze to flow throughout the house.[29]

HO CHI MINH CITY, VIETNAM

Year completed: 2013 | Level of Difficulty: Medium

Climate: Tropical[32] | Key Attribute: Bilateral Massing

Binh Thanh House

Vo Trong Nghia Architects

This house is composed of three volumes that shift back and forth from a terrace to the indoors, with each volume wrapped by punctured concrete blocks. These volumes alternate in order to adapt to the bustling street on one end and the natural river on the other end.

The adjacent outdoor spaces provide a space for residents to enjoy the wind, sun, private gardens, and the scene of the river.[31]

Bahar House
Ayeneh Office

This project adopts a modern principle of creating large open spaces with seamless transitions from one space to another, as opposed to traditional private walled spaces. Multi-use spaces allow for rooms to be used in varied ways during different times of the day.[33]

NAJAFABAD, IRAN

Year completed: 2015 | Level of Difficulty: Easy

Climate: Temperate[34] | Key Attribute: Open Floor Plan

Brick House
Diego Arraigada Arquitecto

This project prioritizes a compact footprint. The use of brickwork is derivative of city regulations, as well as a contextual relationship to the surrounding buildings. The design includes perforations in the masonry, called the English cross lock, to allow light in, and to use a minimal amount of material. Other interior walls are 30-45 cm thick due to this mass they do not need to have waterproof or thermal insulation.[35]

ROSARIO, ARGENTINA

Year completed: 2016 | Level of Difficulty: Medium

Climate: Arid[36] | Key Attribute: Brick

BALI, INDONESIA

Year completed: 2016 | Level of Difficulty: Medium

Climate: Tropical[38] | Key Attribute: Tri Mandala (Nine Regions) Floor Plan

Casablancka Residence

Budi Pradono

This project references traditional Balinese spatial concepts while including modern elements such as the concrete and glass. The concept of "Tri Mandala" (consisting of three realms or nine regions) is used in programming and designing the floor plan of the space. The *akasa* or the center of this nine-region space is left empty providing a moment of pause in a busy household.[37]

SANTA CRUZ, BOLIVIA

Year completed: 2012 | Level of Difficulty: Easy

Climate: Tropical [40] | Key Attribute: Multi-Family Dwelling

Equipetrol Houses

Sommet & Asociados

This project appears to be one larger building, however, consists of two individual homes within a single volume. The homes are similar in floor plan and intersect only at the courtyard. This courtyard contains a swimming pool, where inhabitants of the two homes socialize with each other.[39]

Cuckoo House
Tropical Space Co., Ltd

This project is designed for a family of four and is distinguished by an added program of a coffee shop. The project is built with locally sourced bricks that form the volumes that resemble a "cuckoo clock." The three volumes cater to each category of inhabitants of the house: owners, children, and guests.[41]

DA NANG, VIETNAM

Year completed: 2019 | Level of Difficulty: Medium

Climate: Tropical [42] | Key Attribute: Residential-Commercial Typology

Ger
Community Members

About 800,000 of Mongolia's 2.8 million inhabitants still live the traditional nomadic lifestyle that has remained largely unchanged for generations. This population uses a type of a circular tent-like shelter that can be assembled and disassembled relatively quickly. In 2013, the Mongolian government initiated a portable SHS technology campaign that now allows people living in a Ger to have access to electricty. By simply adding this one feature, nomadic people can use important electronic communication devices. [43]

ULAANBAATAR, MONGOLIA

Year completed: 2013 | Level of Difficulty: Medium

Climate: Mediterranean [44] | Key Attribute: Portable Architecture

BAGHDAD, IRAQ

Year completed: 1937 | Level of Difficulty: Easy

Climate: Desert [46] | Key Attribute: Concrete

Kamil Chadirji Home

Badri Qadah

Located on the east bank of the Tigris River, this project showcases modern developments in the 1940s. The introduction of reinforced concrete into the country at this time led to a design with irregular exterior shapes. The design also consists of a decentralized open interior floor plan.[45]

AMMAN, JORDAN

Year completed: Late 1940s | Level of Difficulty: Difficult

Climate: Desert [48] | Key Attribute: Historical Renovation

Mango House

Mukhtar Saqr

This project is an ancestral home that was remodeled in the 1940s, and still remains in possession of the Mango family. It was originally built with smooth rose stone and wrap-around balconies. The rooms of this house are separated for each program, as opposed to the traditional style of a tripartite plan which divides the house into three more open sections.[47]

Maani Residence

Maisam Architects and Engineers

Designed by, and for, the architect, this house is rooted in local identity through its symbolic reference to Jordanian villages. As a result, the concept is approached with a 30-meter-long corridor extending to the clustered living spaces.[49]

OAK HILL, JORDAN

Year completed: 2003 | Level of Difficulty: Medium

Climate: Mediterranean[50] | Key Attribute: Corridor

Museo Casa Vilamajó

Vilamajó, Pucciarelli & Carve Company

This project was designed to be the architect's familial residence, and exists as an early example of Uruguayan modernism. It features rigorous geometry and brutalist forms broken by playful details on the façade, such as a miniature ship's bows, a lion head medallion, and patterns of colorful circles culminating into Vilamajó's signature eclectic style. It is now used as a museum dedicated to the preservation and exhibition of Julio Vilamajó's works.[51]

MONTEVIDEO, URUGUAY

Year completed: 1930 | Level of Difficulty: Medium

Climate: Tropical[52] | Key Attribute: Preservation

Mussafah Gardens

Rafik El-Khoury & Partners

ABU DHABI, UNITED ARAB EMIRATES

Year completed: 2014 | Level of Difficulty: Medium

Climate: Desert[54] | Key Attribute: High-Density Housing

This project consists of two residential towers of 17 floors each and includes a community center. This complex blends contemporary designs with traditional arabian influences and also includes a mosque within its compounds.[53]

Nowaday Rd

SPINE Architects

YANGON, MYANMAR (BURMA)

Year completed: 2016 | Level of Difficulty: Medium

Climate: Tropical[56] | Key Attribute: Wood

This project utilizes contemporary construction methods while also alluding to traditional Burmese homes by featuring wood posts and wood floor planks. Additional elements, like white interior walls, a new staircase with suspended wooden steps, and a glass railing, modernize the interior space.[55]

Niamey 2000 Housing
Atelier Masomi

This project proposes a model that increases density to counter the city's growth. This project proposed new buildings with two stories, rather than the traditional one story, to increase occupancy per structure. The cultures of multiple units as opposed to a high-rise, also maintain a known level of comfort the locals have acclimated to when it comes to their built environment. The project also prioritizes efficient architectural systems such as passive cooling techniques and locally sourced materials.[57]

NIAMEY, NIGER

Year completed: 1930 | Level of Difficulty: Medium

Climate: Temperate[58] | Key Attribute: Housing Complex

Pajarera House
Catalina Patiño + Viviana Peña

The house is situated in the hilly woodland of the Aburrá Valley, on a sloped portion of the site. It resembles a palafito (stilt house), one of Chile's traditional housing typologies. Due to the placement of the home and terrace, plants and water are able to pass under the house.[59]

NIAMEY, NIGER

Year completed: 1930 | Level of Difficulty: Easy

Climate: Tropical[60] | Key Attribute: Stilt House

UNKNOWN, KUWAIT

Year completed: 2020 | Level of Difficulty: Medium

Climate: Desert [62] | Key Attribute: Hosh

Ternion 3 Villas

Studio Toggle

Three independent villas variably stacked to create a porous, pixelated massing to balance privacy with the community. Each villa centers around a private courtyard that includes a swimming pool. This swimming pool is an attempt to reinterpret the concept of a Hosh (a traditional Arabic water feature in a courtyard space). Full-height windows allow for cross ventilation and evaporative cooling. The cantilevered volumes, due to the stacking of villas, allow for shade.[61]

QUANG NGAI, VIETNAM

Year completed: 2019 | Level of Difficulty: Easy

Climate: Tropical [64] | Key Attribute: Roof Garden

The Red Roof House

TAA Design

This project is located in an area that is experiencing rapid urbanization. In traditional Vietnamese landscapes, the "red roof" house is a common typology. In order to adapt this typology to higher density developments, this project utilizes a stepped roof that reduces the height of the façade to ensure that it does not overpower its surroundings. This roof also serves as a vegetable garden to regulate the interior temperature by cooling the home and to generate social interactions with the community.[63]

The Grey House
Paradigm DH

This project is a single-family private residence with a backyard and a pool. The gradient of privacy decreases as inhabitants move up the building. The lower level consists of public and large group entertainment spaces such as the salon, while the upper level consists of private bedrooms. This organization of privacy is also reflected in the façade as the front of the building consists of fewer openings while the back has larger windows that face the yard and pool.[65]

AMMAN, JORDAN

Year completed: 2020 | Level of Difficulty: Difficult

Climate: Arid[66] | Key Attribute: Bilateral Characteristics

A Typical Shophouse
Things Matter

This project is a redesign of the Bangkok shop-house typology. The plumbing and the staircase are moved toward the center of the house to allow for cross-ventilation throughout the building. Large windows are strategically placed at both ends of the small unit to allow for cross ventilation and sunlight in a small space.[67]

BANGKOK, THAILAND

Year completed: 2010 | Level of Difficulty: Easy

Climate: Tropical[68] | Key Attribute: Micro Unit

AL ALAMAYN, EGYPT

Year completed: 2014 | Level of Difficulty: Medium

Climate: Desert [70] | Key Attribute: Passive Cooling

Al Alfy House
Shahira Famy Architects

This project utilizes passive cooling techniques due to the heat and humidity of its surrounding environment. Facing windows promote cross ventilation to achieve thermal comfort and allow light to enter throughout the building. A terracotta roof and white stone walls clad the structure on a pre-existing column grid.[69]

NOSARA, COSTA RICA

Year completed: Unknown | Level of Difficulty: Medium

Climate: Tropical [72] |Key Attribute: Indoor-Outdoor Concept

Casa Jade
Prendas Loria

This project's architectural elements are focused on making this space ideal for its primary purpose—to practice yoga and to interact with flora around the site. It utilizes an indoor outdoor concept around a central courtyard that creates pathways for passive cooling. The materials used, such as concrete and light woods, also help to control the temperature of the interior. Additionally, the shape of the roof provides protection from heavy rains, while allowing for a light and breeze.[71]

Casa MD
Atelier Vidal

This project utilizes an indoor-outdoor concept as it is situated in a tropical climate. The upper floor's façade consists of operable timber-clad screens that help regulate the amount of air and light penetrating the private spaces. Public spaces within this U-shaped building open toward a central courtyard and its 25m lap pool.[73]

KINGSTON, JAMAICA

Year completed: 2017 | Level of Difficulty: Difficult

Climate: Tropical[74] | Key Attribute: Timber Screen

Dar Mabruka
Jack Ishkanes

This project aims to adapt modern architectural principles to Sudanese culture and climate. The interior is designed to be naturally ventilated by placing large openings near the ground and smaller openings below the ceiling. Involving local craftsmen is integral to the project as the balustrades, hinges, and pots were made in Omdurman by boat makers, ironmongers, and other craftsmen around the Nile. The lampshades for the project are inspired by regional baskets or gufa.[75]

KHARTOUM, SUDAN

Year completed: 1990 | Level of Difficulty: Medium

Climate: Desert[76] | Key Attribute: Local Craftsmanship

ASSINIE-MAFIA, CÔTE D'IVOIRE

Year completed: 2004 | Level of Difficulty: Difficult

Climate: Arid [78] | Key Attribute: Indoor-Outdoor Living

Ebrah Pavillion
Koffi & Diabaté

This project utilizes an indoor-outdoor plan to create interconnected spaces between rooms and patio areas. Spaces such as the dining area and lounge area are all located outside, adjacent to the pool. This layout also creates an easy flow for passive cooling techniques [systems to occur]. This project is a part of the firm's larger efforts in the city of Assinie-Mafia that is focussed on eco-friendly solutions for developing along the coast.[77]

ST. ANDREW, JAMAICA

Year completed: Unknown | Level of Difficulty: Difficult

Climate: Tropical [80] | Key Attribute: Retirement Home

Garraway Residence
Form Architects

This is a small retirement home designed for an elderly couple. Located on a plateau, the house has multiple views of the blue mountain peaks. The house is completely solar powered, and utilizes a rainwater harvesting system. Additionally, outdoor deck spaces like the roof terrace and the balconies allow the occupants to observe the surrounding landscape.[79]

El Avila
SDH Studio

EL AVILA NATIONAL PARK, VENEZUELA

Year completed: Unknown | Level of Difficulty: Medium

Climate: Tropical[82] | Key Attribute: Inverted Roof

Set on the mountains of El Avila National Park, this family home offers spectacular views. The locally sourced stone, and a curved wood ceiling, create a dynamic contrast to the minimalistic straight lines of the building envelope. An inverted corrugated steel roof is used to harvest rainwater, due to the lack of natural water in this remote National Park.[81]

House on a Rock
Bruce Rowland Architects, Muzia Sforza, Studio Seilern

ZIMBABWE

Year completed: 2012 | Level of Difficulty: Easy

Climate: Temperate[84] | Key Attribute: Cantilever Structure

The structure of the project consists of oversized cantilever roofs and extensive terrace, making the building appear as if it is floating above the rock that it rests on. Two granite blocks anchor the building into the rock, and two glass boxes span between the deck and roof enclosing the winter living areas. All materials were sourced locally except for speciality items, and all excavation for construction is still displayed within the site.[83]

UNQILLO, ARGENTINA

Year completed: 2016 | Level of Difficulty: Easy

Climate: Temperate[86] | Key Attribute: Stone Outcrop

JB House
Alarcia Ferrer Arquitectos

Located in a quarry area, the land has numerous outcrops of stone that leave unique imprints on the landscape. Two important outcrops are used to form part of the domestic and intimate plan of the house. These act as anchors for the house as well as an external texture to the interior.[85]

SRI JAYEWARDENEPURA, SRI LANKA

Year completed: 2014 | Level of Difficulty: Medium

Climate: Tropical[88] | Key Attribute: Garden View

Permeable House at Sri Jayawardenapura Kotte
Palinda Kannangara Architects

The project is a rectilinear building with windows and other apertures that face the garden that surrounds the site. It utilizes a double-screen fenestration system that is used as a shading device to regulate sunlight in varied living spaces given the climatic conditions.[87]

Master Bungalow
Vanuatu Builders

This home is made with a timber frame construction and concrete posts. The roof structure is composed of a natangura plant fiber over roof battens over a waterproof membrane over 12mm ply. A ventilation opening right beneath the thatched roof is kept permanently open. The interior rooms of this home include bedrooms and bathrooms, while the porch is laid out for activities such as cooking and lounging.[89]

PORT VILA, VANUATU

Year completed: Unknown | Level of Difficulty: Medium

Climate: Tropical[90] | Key Attribute: Thatched Roof

Takuru House
José Cubilla & Asociados

The goal of this project was to create an affordable, and environmentally resilient house that sources 85% of its material from its site. The excavated pit used to gather raw materials was later used as a water reservoir for livestock. The bricks that were subsequently made, helped the project achieve adequate temperatures within the house. The project also makes use of other lower tech and inventive solutions for climate control and waste management.[91]

PIRIBEBUY, PARAGUAY

Year completed: 2016 | Level of Difficulty: Medium

Climate: Tropical[92] | Key Attribute: Regional Building Strategies

LAGOS, NIGERIA

Year completed: 2019 | Level of Difficulty: Easy

Climate: Tropical[94] | Key Attribute: Beach House

Sencillo Beach House
cmDesign Atelier

The objective of this project is to create multiple gathering and entertaining spaces. This project is made from locally sourced materials like cedar wood and white concerte. The house utilizes minimalist modern elements, which are juxtaposed with a steel screen that is inspired by geometry found in regional art. This privacy screen also acts as a shading system that reduces the sun's glare.[93]

SANTA CRUZ, BOLIVIA

Year completed: 2012 | Level of Difficulty: Easy

Climate: Tropical[96] | Key Attribute: Multi-Family Dwelling

Women's Dormitory & Meditation Building, Wat Pa Wachirabanpot
Walllasia

This project is a mediation center with housing accommodations for female dharma practitioners. The project is placed in alignment to the locations longitudes to provide distinct views of the forest from every room. The foundation was built using soil from a nearby pond that holds potable water, and provides a soothing view for the residents. This project utilizes courtyards with open corridors to create an indoor-outdoor concept.[95]

Westworld Way Private Residence
MMA Design Studio

PARKVIEW, JOHANNESBURG, SOUTH AFRICA

Year completed: 2016 | Level of Difficulty: Medium

Climate: Tropical [98] | Key Attribute: Multi-Family Dwelling

This project is designed to be a dwelling for two families. The house intersects at the central courtyard and communal kitchen. The courtyard entrances for both the houses consist of sliding doors. Additionally, the two dwellings are located on a sloping site. This is used as an opportunity to create a mountain-like landscape that overlooks different spaces within the project.[97]

Yaba Prototype
NLÉ architects

LAGOS, NIGERIA

Year completed: N/A | Level of Difficulty: Medium

Climate: Tropical [100] | Key Attribute: Modular

The Yaba Prototype is a housing prototype for rapidly urbanizing spaces. This project is a dense and self-sufficient housing block. The design of this prototype allows for housing units to be combined as needed, which gives flexibility to respond to the variable need of the market. The building block can also be adapted for offices, recreational, institutional, and other uses creating a "city within a building" model.[99]

KUTCH, INDIA

Year completed: 2003 | Level of Difficulty: Easy

Climate: Arid[110] | Key Attribute: Village-Reconstruction

Rehabilitation of Bhadli Village
SNK

The project focuses on rebuilding a village in Kutch following a natural disaster. As villagers refused government proposed uniform housing, SNK along with their client took this case as a pro-bono project. The villagers were employed as construction workers to combat unemployment and SNK supplied materials for free. This not only gave the locals a source of income but also the freedom to personalize their homes. As a result, a total of 124 homes were built. A women's center was also built to boost the crafting output of the village.[109]

CHITRA, PAKISTAN

Year completed: 2015 | Level of Difficulty: Easy

Climate: Arid[112] | Key Attribute: Octagonal Structure

Lari OctaGreen
Lari Associates

This project was designed in response to the October 2015 earthquake in Pakistan that destroyed the homes of 160 families. This new shelter typology, in an octagonal form, creates a DRR compliant structure, and an additional mud exterior prevents the shelter from overturning, and acts as insulation. Additionally, this project uses locally sourced materials and construction methods, creating a zero carbon footprint.[111]

Sangamam Cost-Efficient Habitat
Anupama Kundoo Architects

Sangamam is an area affected by water scarcity, saline water intrusion, soil erosion, declining soil fertility, and inadequate housing. In response to these issues, a low-cost housing scheme was proposed to provide eco-friendly building infrastructure for rainwater harvesting with terracotta filter slabs and wastewater treatment systems.[113]

AUROVILLE, INDIA

Year completed: 1973 | Level of Difficulty: Medium

Climate: Tropical[114] | Key Attribute: Affordable Housing

Troglodyte House
Residents

Troglodyte homes are built by excavating a deep circular pit into the sandstone with simple hand tools, followed by caves dug out to form underground rooms. The main pit is used as a courtyard space while the cave-like rooms offer an escape from the heat of the day. Due to many rebuilds in the 1960s post flooding, some are able to be retrofitted with technology. While still in a very rural area, many are now surrounded by highways and border modern homes.[115]

JEBEL DAHAR REGION, TUNISIA

Year completed: 1960s | Level of Difficulty: Easy

Climate: Desert [116] | Key Attribute: Pit-Housing

CHENNAI, TAMIL NADU, INDIA

Year completed: 2012 | Level of Difficulty: Difficult

Climate: Tropical[118] | Key Attribute: Art Commune

Cholamandal Artists Village
Shilpa Architects and M. V. Devan

This project is acclaimed as among the most successful and surviving art communes in the world. The construction for this project started in 1996 and continued to expand to 10 acres over 16 years.
The buildings within this commune are largely constructed with brick and concrete and the additional use of plaster and paint was avoided.
The galleries in these buildings open toward the landscape and flora of the site.[117]

KARATU, TANZANIA

Year completed: 2018 | Level of Difficulty: Medium

Climate: Temperate[120] | Key Attribute: Dormitory

Black Rhino Academy: Dormitories
NLÉ

This international boarding school is situated near the Ngorongoro Conservation Area and is designed to create a learning environment that interacts with nature. The campus master plan is inspired by the Masai Boma settlements—a planning principle vested in the region for millennia. In this type of development, the building units are arranged radially, the homes are placed on the interior while the outermost ring consists of thorn bushes that act as a protective barrier for the farmland and settlements.[119]

El Rancho
MBAD Architects

This project is located in a seaside area and draws inspiration from a summer ranch typology. It was designed to be an affordable housing solution that makes use of traditional local materials, such as brick. The residents were encouraged to design their own floor plans as per their needs, and they were able to transform this set to include multi-use spaces, similar to micro-units. Additionally, 50% of the project can be constructed by manual labor of the residents, thus lowering construction costs.[121]

HERMOSA BEACH, URUGUAY

Year completed: 2014 | Level of Difficulty: Difficult

Climate: Temperate[122] | Key Attribute: Affordable Housing

Gando Teachers' Housing
Kere-Architecture

These homes were built to attract teachers and their families to the countryside. They are a series of adaptable modules comparable in size to traditional round huts in the region. The simplicity in the design means it is easily adaptable in various ways for the residents. The materials used in this project are sustainable and locally sourced earth blocks, as well as some concrete.[123]

GANDO, BURKINA FASO

Year completed: 2004 | Level of Difficulty: Easy

Climate: Tropical[124] | Key Attribute: Teachers' Housing

SÃO PAULO, BRAZIL

Year completed: 2013 | Level of Difficulty: Medium

Climate: Tropical [126] | Key Attribute: Public Amenities

Jardim Edite
MMBB, H+ F Arquitectos

This project dedicates its ground level to public programs like a culinary school, a healthcare center, and a nursery to serve the surrounding community. This integrates the building in the larger economic and social urban fabric of its site. The housing program exists vertically above this public space. Housing buildings connect within each block, allowing for a secluded place for social interaction between the residents.[125]

APAN, MÉXICO

Year completed: 2017 | Level of Difficulty: Difficult

Climate: Temperate [128] | Key Attribute: Affordable Housing

House 8, Apan Housing Laboratory
Taller Mauricio Rocha + Gabriela Carrillo

This Apan Housing Laboratory Project investigates affordable housing typologies in Mexico. Situated in this Laboratory, House 8 uses vernacular materials (CMU, adobe, wood) and construction techniques in two volumes. A portico at the intersection of these volumes acts as a connection between the two distinct areas, and allows for future expansion of the volumes if necessary. The horizontal volume made of CMU's, houses social spaces, and the vertical volume made of adobe, houses private programs.[127]

LGBTQ Youth Asylum Center
Marcelo Venzon, Julia Park, Guilherme Pardini and João Paulo Carrascoza

This project is designed by second prize winners of the LGBTQ Youth Asylum Center, a competition organized by Bee Breeders. The design consists of a structure held in tension and linked together with a cable that supports a wire mesh, and covered with a flexible membrane. The proposed project also consists of five different gardens that are utilized as reflection spaces for its visitors.[129]

UGANDA

Year completed: 2013 | Level of Difficulty: Medium

Climate: Tropical[130] | Key Attribute: LGBTQ Center

Mabushi Medium-Density Residential
NLÉ architects

This project is a part of a series of medium-density homes located in a rapidly developing middle income district, designed to maximize land area. The dense housing provides terraces for each unit. It also consists of community spaces for a larger group of its residents to gather in.[131]

ABUJA, NIGERIA

Year completed: 2013 | Level of Difficulty: Medium

Climate: Tropical[132] | Key Attribute: Medium-Density Housing

ACCRA, GHANA

Year completed: Unknown | Level of Difficulty: Difficult

Climate: Tropical[134] | Key Attribute: Rammed Earth

Pata4two

Orthner Orthner & Associates

This project creates new affordable housing that draws inspiration from pata—or a traditional form of housing in the region. Construction details include a rammed earth foundation to reduce the amount of cement almost completely, while improving the indoor climate. It also incorporates new technologies to embrace the needs of a growing middle class. It includes both lower tech solutions such as rainwater harvesting, as well as higher tech solutions such as a bio-digester for the toilet waste.[133]

KIGALI, KICUKIRO DISTRICT, RWANDA

Year completed: 2017 | Level of Difficulty: Medium

Climate: Tropical[136] | Key Attribute: Sustainable Housing

Masaka Affordable Housing

MASS Design Group

This project addresses Rwanda's growing urban population that seeks affordable housing. In addition this project is designed to have a carbon footprint that is 57% less than the national average. This building comprises numerous housing layouts that are able to accommodate various family sizes. By incorporating communal areas such as storages for market produce, laundry facilities, vegetable gardens or *akarima k'igikoni*, and event spaces the residents and their neighbors have the opportunity to strengthen their community.[135]

Prototype Housing
Collective Studio

This proposal of the "Big Roof House" focuses on providing shaded outdoor spaces as opposed to close knit indoor spaces. Partnering with Habitat for Humanity Cambodia, the firm was tasked to create six alternatives to low-cost housing that address varying needs. They improved passive cooling methods by remodeling the traditional brick house to instead use a lightweight timber frame, fiber cement sheeting, and concrete slab floor. The project was also developed with maximum local community involvement in both its design phase and build phase.[137]

MULTIPLE SEMI-URBAN SITES, CAMBODIA

Year completed: 2011-2013 | Level of Difficulty: Medium

Climate: Tropical[138] | Key Attribute: Lightweight Structure

Quinta Monroy
Elemental

This project was built to provide homes for 100 families in the Chilean desert. The project rehoused residents in their existing central location that they had been living in since the 1960s. This empowered the families socially and economically by continuing their same access to work, education, and the city. To make the project affordable, the essentials of the home, such as the kitchen, bathroom, stairs, etc., were proposed as a design build project. Each unit also includes an empty space, so the family can expand their home.[139]

IQUIQUE, CHILE

Year completed: 2004 | Level of Difficulty: Easy

Climate: Arid[140] | Key Attribute: Social Housing

LAGOS, NIGERIA

Year completed: 2017 | Level of Difficulty: Medium

Climate: Tropical[142] | Key Attribute: Modern Façade

The Plum Apartments
cmDesign Atelier

This project is designed for young professionals in the trendy neighborhood of Osapa who are looking for relatively modern accommodations. To suit its audience, a vibrant red is juxtaposed with a gray and white façade. Each building also features a courtyard that allows light to flood through each building and creates opportunities for passive ventilation.[141]

GANDO, BURKINA FASO

Year completed: Under construction | Level of Difficulty: Medium

Climate: Arid[144] | Key Attribute: Earthen Pot Storage

Songtaaba Women's Center
Kere Architecture

This project caters to two primary functions: to provide sheltered space for women and to provide larger weather-proof storage spaces. The storage of the building allows women to store grains they harvest and sell it for profit. Grains are stored in hand-made pottery produced locally by the women. The sheltered space is built with clay walls, and a concrete platform elevated by a series of concrete pilotis.[143]

Villa for Girls
Soliscolomer y Asociados

TEGUCIGALPA, HONDURAS

Year completed: 2013 | Level of Difficulty: Medium

Climate: Tropical[146] | Key Attribute: Educational Facility

This project was designed as a small villa that primarily offers education to girls and was developed in association with Sisters of Mary's education efforts. The goal of this organization is to raise socially responsible individuals who will return to their communities and help their local community members grow and prosper. Thus, this proposal focuses on providing holistic growth for the kids by also incorporating recreational spaces like walking trails, a gym, workshop spaces, and dormitories.[145]

The Viviendas del Hogar de Cristo (CHD) project
Jorge Moran Ubidia & Jesuit Priests

GUAYAQUIL, ECUADOR

Year completed: 1996-Present | Level of Difficulty: Medium

Climate: Tropical[148] | Key Attribute: Sustainable and Affordable Housing

This project is a series of environmentally friendly, affordable homes for low-income families. The dwellings are made of bamboo and prefabricated panels, they are easy to construct, a family can build their own in a day. The houses look similar to the ones that people built themselves when land was first acquired, but are longer lasting. The perform well in the humid climate, and many are raised above ground level due to flooding.[147]

Woldyia Maternity Center
Vilalta Arquitectura

This project is developed as housing for those about to give birth and traveling from rural areas. The project is divided into two halves that share the same entrance, one is the maternity unit, and the other is a waiting area. The design of the façade includes traditional Ethiopian textile patterns on the window grills.[150]

WOLDYIA, ETHIOPIA

Year completed: 2017 | Level of Difficulty: Easy

Climate: Arid[149] | Key Attribute: Maternity Home

Citations

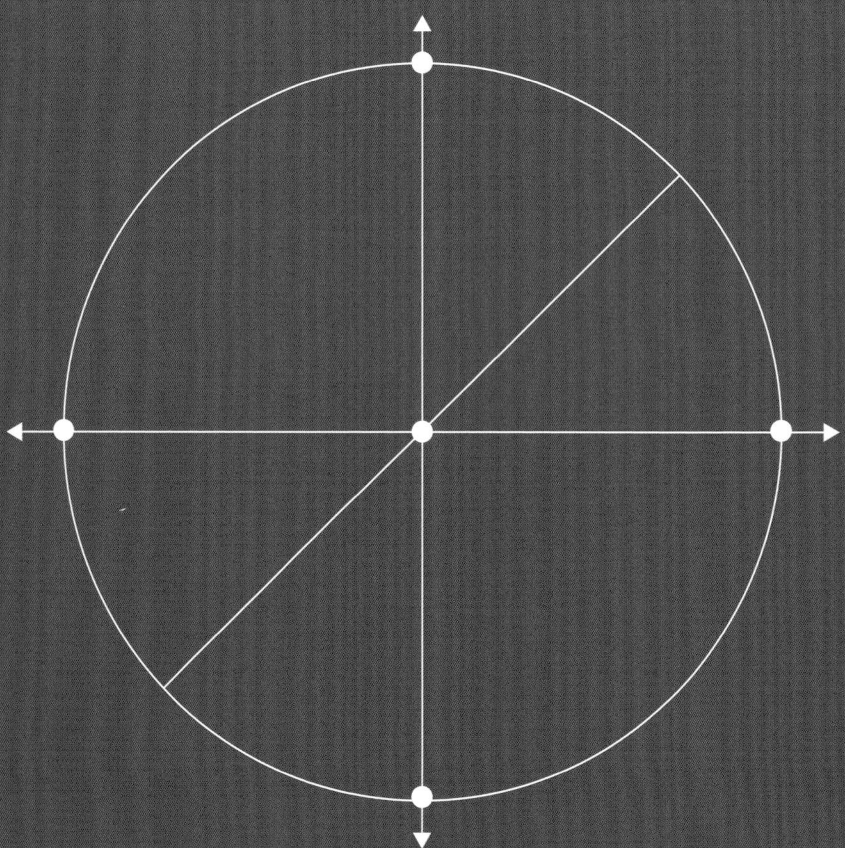

1. Sánchez, Daniel. "Ancon Building / Irene Joselevich + Ana Rascovsky + Billy Gutraich." ArchDaily. ArchDaily, April 21, 2015. https://www.archdaily.com/621675/edificio-ancon-irene-joselevich-ana-rascovsky-billy-gutraich.

2. "Data.org." Climate. Accessed August 30, 2022. https://en.climate-data.org/south-america/argentina/buenos-aires-161/.

3. "Casa Cinco Patios." Plantastudio. Accessed August 31, 2022. https://www.estudioplanta.com/cincopatios. Casa Cinco Patios: Mena, Florencia. "Casa Cinco Patios / Ana Rascovsky Arqs." ArchDaily. ArchDaily, July 21, 2016. https://www.archdaily.com/791545/casa-cinco-patios-ana-rascovsky-arqs?ad_medium=office_landing&ad_name=article.

4. "Data.org." Climate. Accessed August 31, 2022. https://en.climate-data.org/south-america/argentina/buenos-aires-161/.

5. "Extension of Identity." Paseo Architecture, July 30, 2020. https://paseoarch.com/portfolio/extension-of-identity/.

6. "Data.org." Climate. Accessed August 31, 2022. https://en.climate-data.org/asia/lebanon-50/.

7. Eleanor Gibson | 2 September 2017 1 comment. "White Latticed Screens Encase Apartment Block in Kenya by Urko Sanchez." Dezeen, January 27, 2022. https://www.dezeen.com/2017/09/02/tudor-apartments-housing-architecture-urko-sanchez-architects-mombasa-kenya/.
Swahili Gem Apartments: "Swahili Gem." Urko, December 27, 2021. https://urkosanchez.com/work/swahili-gem-apartments/.

8. "Climate-Kenya." Kenya climate: average weather, temperature, precipitation, when to go. Accessed August 31, 2022. https://www.climatestotravel.com/climate/kenya.

9. AGI Architects. Wind Tower. AGI Architects, June 1, 2022. https://www.agi-architects.com/en/work/wind-tower/.
Wind Tower: Sagredo, Rayen. "Wind Tower / AGI Architects." ArchDaily. ArchDaily, July 25, 2017. https://www.archdaily.com/876432/wind-tower-agi-architects.

10. "Climate: Kuwait." Climate-Data.Org. Climate-Data.Org. Accessed September 4, 2022. https://en.climate-data.org/asia/kuwait-125/.

11. Casa Aguirre, Pablo. "Galpon House by 2172 / Asociados in Chile." Architecture Art Designs. Archi Art Designs, October 12, 2021. https://www.architectureartdesigns.com/galpon-house-by-2172-asociados-in-chile/.
Tapia, Daniel. "Galpón House / 2172 / Asociados." ArchDaily. ArchDai-

ly, January 16, 2020. https://www.archdaily.com/931954/casa-galpon-2172-asociados.

12. Climate Data Org. "Climate Lago Rapel." Climate Data Org. Climate Data Org. Accessed September 1, 2022. https://en.climate-data.org/south-america/chile/x-region-de-los-lagos-75/.

13. Abdel, Hana. "Game Lodge / Slee & Co Architects." ArchDaily. ArchDaily, May 21, 2020. https://www.archdaily.com/939351/the-hunting-lodge-slee-and-co-architects?ad_source=search&ad_medium=search_result_all.

14. Sebastian, Info Namibia. "Climate and Weather of Namibia." Namibia Travel. Info Namibia. Accessed September 1, 2022. https://www.info-namibia.com/info/namibia-weather.

15. Dulanto, Martin. "Casa Topo." Martin Dulanto Arquitecto. Martin Dulanto Arquitecto. Accessed September 1, 2022. https://martindulanto.com/proyecto/casa-topo.
Topo House: Caballero, Pilar. "Topo House / Martin Dulanto Arquitecto." ArchDaily. ArchDaily, February 12, 2019. https://www.archdaily.com/910882/topo-house-martin-dulanto-arquitecto.

16. Climate Data Org. "Clima Lima." Climate Data Org. Climate Data Org. Accessed September 1, 2022. https://en.climate-data.org/south-america/peru/lima/lima-1014/.

17. Winston, Anna. "Tropical Box House Is Wrapped in a Concrete 'Egg-Crate.' Dezeen. Dezeen, September 5, 2022. https://www.dezeen.com/2015/09/05/tropical-box-house-kuala-lumpur-malaysia-whbc-architects-wrapped-concrete-egg-crate-stilts/.
Tropical Box House: Aguilar, Cristian. Tropical Box House / WHBC Architects." ArchDaily. ArchDaily, May 27, 2015. https://www.archdaily.com/635387/house-tropical-box-whbc-architects.

18. Encyclopædia Britannica. "Climate of Malaysia." Encyclopædia Britannica. Encyclopædia Britannica, Inc. Accessed September 1, 2022. https://www.britannica.com/place/Malaysia/Climate.

19. Villa Saxo: Studio Saxe. "Villa Saxo." Studio Saxe. Studio Saxe, February 4, 2020. https://studiosaxe.com/projects/villa-saxo/.

20. Climate Data Org. "Climate Guanacaste." Climate Data Org. Climate Data Org. Accessed September 1, 2022. https://en.climate-data.org/north-america/costa-rica/guanacaste-1004/.

21. Caballero, Pilar. "House in the Páramo / Zita." ArchDaily. ArchDaily, November 26, 2021. https://www.archdaily.com/972484/house-in-the-paramo-zita?ad_source=search&ad_

medium=projects_tab.

22. "Climate of Colombia." Encyclopædia Britannica. Encyclopædia Britannica, inc. Accessed September 1, 2022. https://www.britannica.com/place/Colombia/Climate.

23. Walls and butterflies. Accessed September 1, 2022. http://kvadratinterwoven.com/walls-and-butterflies. Bioclimatic Prototype of a Host and NEctar Garden Building: Fracalossi, Igor. "Bioclimatic Prototype of a Host and Nectar Garden Building / Husos Architects." ArchDaily. ArchDaily, August 21, 2015. https://www.archdaily.com/772039/bioclimatic-prototype-of-a-host-and-nectar-garden-building-husos.

24. "Climate of Colombia." Encyclopædia Britannica. Encyclopædia Britannica, Inc. Accessed September 1, 2022. https://www.britannica.com/place/Colombia/Climate.

25. "Plan B Guatemala: Deoc Arquitectos." Archello. Accessed September 1, 2022. https://archello.com/project/plan-b-guatemala. Plan B: Tapia, Daniel. "Plan B Guatemala / DEOC Arquitectos." ArchDaily. ArchDaily, March 12, 2021. https://www.archdaily.com/910416/plan-b-guatemala-deoc-arquitectos.

26. "Data.org." Climate. Accessed September 1, 2022. https://en.climate-data.org/north-america/guatemala/escuintla/el-paredon-873435/.

27. Urko Sanchez Architects. "Sos Childrens' Village." Urko. Urko Sanchez Architects, December 12, 2021. https://urkosanchez.com/work/sos-childrens-village-tadjourah-djibouti.
SOS Childrens Village: Aguilar, Cristian. "SOS Children's Village in Djibouti / Urko Sanchez Architects." ArchDaily. December 2, 2020. https://www.archdaily.com/773319/sos-childrens-village-in-djibouti-urko-sanchez-architects. Stevens, Philip. "Urko Sanchez Designs a Car-Free Village for Children in Djibouti." Designboom, January 27, 2016. https://www.designboom.com/architecture/urko-sanchez-architects-sos-childrens-village-in-djibouti-12-06-2015

28. Climate Data Org. "Data.org." Climate. Climate Data Org. Accessed August 31, 2022. https://en.climate-data.org/africa/djibouti/tadjourah/tadjoura-31637/.

29. "Alma El Shaab House." Almimariya. Almimariya, 2018. http://www.almimariya.com/projects/residential/alma-el-shaab-house/.

30. "Climate-Data.org." Climate-Data.org. Accessed August 30, 2022. https://en.climate-data.org/asia/lebanon-50/.

31. McDougall, Ella. "The Binh Thanh House in Vietnam: Habitus Living." Habitusliving.com, November 20, 2017. https://www.habitusliving.com/

architecture/binh-thanh-house-vietnam.

32. "Data.org." Climate. Accessed August 31, 2022. https://en.climate-data.org/asia/vietnam/ho-chi-minh-city-840/.

33. Sánchez, Daniel. "Bahar House / Ayeneh Office." ArchDaily. ArchDaily, January 3, 2016. https://www.archdaily.com/779679/bahar-house-ayeneh-office.

34. "Data.org." Climate. Accessed August 31, 2022. https://en.climate-data.org/asia/iran-66/.

35. Tapia, Daniel. "Brick House / Diego Arraigada Arquitecto." ArchDaily. ArchDaily, November 19, 2019. https://www.archdaily.com/928661/brick-house-diego-arraigada-arquitectos?ad_source=search&ad_medium=search_result_projects.
Brick House: Additional Source: Bardelli. Diego Arraigada Arquitectos. Accessed August 31, 2022. http://diegoarraigada.com/es/trabajos/v/28.

36. "Data.org." Climate. Accessed August 31, 2022. https://en.climate-data.org/south-america/uruguay-191/.

37. Sagredo, Rayen. "Casablancka Residence / Budi Pradono Architects." ArchDaily. ArchDaily, June 20, 2017. https://www.archdaily.com/874030/casablancka-residence-budi-pradono-architects.

38. "Data.org." Climate. Accessed August 31, 2022. https://en.climate-data.org/asia/indonesia/bali/bali-denpasar-3427/.

39. Sánchez, Daniel. "Equipetrol Houses / Sommet & Asociados." ArchDaily. ArchDaily, April 2, 2013. https://www.archdaily.com/353357/equipetrol-houses-sommet-asociados.
Equipetrol Houses: "Equipetrol Houses by Sommet Architects." Architizer, August 8, 2016. https://architizer.com/projects/equipetrol-houses/.

40. "Data.org." Climate. Accessed August 31, 2022. https://en.climate-data.org/south-america/bolivia/santa-cruz/santa-cruz-de-la-sierra-4439/.

41. Architecture, Tropical Space | Vietnam. "Works." Cuckoo Coffee House. Accessed August 31, 2022. https://tropicalspaceil.com/du-an/cuckoo-coffee-house/385.html.
Cuckoo House: "Cuckoo House by Tropical Space." Architizer, June 4, 2020. https://architizer.com/projects/cuckoo-house/.

42. "Climate and Average Monthly Weather in Da Nang (Da Nang Municipality), Vietnam." World Weather & Climate Information. Accessed August 31, 2022. https://weather-and-climate.com/average-monthly-Rainfall-Temperature-Sunshine,-da-nang,Vietnam.

43. Stewart, Philippa H. "Mongolia Going Solar." Environment | Al

Jazeera. Al Jazeera, December 16, 2013. https://www.aljazeera.com/features/2013/12/16/mongolias-nomads-warm-to-solar-power/.

44. "Climate and Average Weather in Mongolia." World Weather & Climate Information. Accessed August 31, 2022. https://weather-and-climate.com/average-monthly-Rainfall-Temperature-Sunshine-in-Mongolia.

45. Kamil Chadirji Housebaghdad, Iraq." Archnet > Site > Kamil Chadirji House. Accessed August 31, 2022. https://www.archnet.org/sites/2813.

46. "Data.org." Climate. Accessed August 31, 2022. https://en.climate-data.org/asia/iraq-146/.

47. "Mango House. Art Destination Jordan, Amman." Universes in Universe-Worlds of Art. Accessed August 31, 2022. https://universes.art/en/art-destinations/jordan/amman/tours/10/mango-house.

48. "Climate of Jordan." Encyclopædia Britannica. Encyclopædia Britannica, Inc. Accessed August 31, 2022. https://www.britannica.com/place/Jordan/Climate.

49. "Maani Residence." maisam. Accessed August 31, 2022. http://maisam.com.jo/content/maani-residence?position=4&list=PCw9K3aGcFmNZcMVp6cAOajP2_X4r-G-B10qgFMMBQ4.

50. "Climate of Jordan." Encyclopædia Britannica. Encyclopædia Britannica, inc. Accessed August 31, 2022. https://www.britannica.com/place/Jordan/Climate.

51. Maiztegui, Belén. "Latin American Architects Who Designed Their Own Houses." ArchDaily. ArchDaily, January 2, 2020. https://www.archdaily.com/930661/latin-american-architects-who-designed-their-own-houses?ad_source=search&ad_medium=search_result_all.

52. "Data.org." Climate. Accessed August 31, 2022. https://en.climate-data.org/south-america/uruguay-191/.

53. "Mussafah Gardens." Fouad Hanna & Associates. Accessed August 31, 2022. http://fouadhanna.com/project/mussafah-garden/.
Mussafah Gardens: "Mussafah Gardens Building Guide." Bayut. Accessed August 31, 2022. https://www.bayut.com/buildings/mussafah-gardens/.

54. "Data.org." Climate. Accessed August 31, 2022. https://en.climate-data.org/asia/united-arab-emirates-70/.

55. Livingasean. "Contemporary House in Myanmar // Living Asean." LIVING ASEAN-Inspiring Tropical Lifestyle //, September 9, 2019. https://livingasean.com/house/contemporary-house-myanmar/.

56. "Climate: Myanmar." Climate-Data.org. Climate-Data.org. Accessed September 4, 2022. https://en.climate-data.org/asia/myanmar-151/.

57. "Niamey 2000." atelier masomi. Accessed August 31, 2022. http://www.ateliermasomi.com/test.
Niamey 2000: Tapia, Daniel. "Niamey 2000 / united4design." ArchDaily. ArchDaily, February 9, 2021. https://www.archdaily.com/875897/niamey-2000-united4design.a

58. "Data.org." Climate. Accessed August 31, 2022. https://en.climate-data.org/africa/niger/niamey/niamey-497/.

59. Mena, Florencia. "Pajarera House / Catalina Patiño + Viviana Peña." ArchDaily. ArchDaily, July 8, 2016. https://www.archdaily.com/790917/pajarera-house-catalina-patino-plus-viviana-pena?ad_source=search&ad_medium=search_result_projects.

60. "Data.org." Climate. Accessed August 31, 2022. https://en.climate-data.org/south-america/colombia/antioquia-72/.

61. "Ternion." Studio Toggle. Accessed August 31, 2022. https://studiotoggle.com/portfolio/completed/ternion.

62. "Data.org." Climate. Accessed August 31, 2022. https://en.climate-data.org/asia/kuwait-125/.

63. Designboom, Philip Stevens I. "A Stepped Garden Provides Produce for the Residents of the Red Roof House in Vietnam." designboom, June 24, 2021. https://www.designboom.com/architecture/taa-design-red-roof-house-vegetable-garden-vietnam-11-10-2019/.

64. "Climate and Average Monthly Weather in Ho Chi Minh City (Ho Chi Minh Municipality), Vietnam." World Weather & Climate Information. Accessed August 31, 2022. https://weather-and-climate.com/average-monthly-Rainfall-Temperature-Sunshine,Ho-Chi-Minh-city,Vietnam.

65. "The Grey House." Paradigm DH, July 3, 2022. https://paradigmdh.com/work/the-grey-house/.

66. "Climate of Jordan." Encyclopædia Britannica. Encyclopædia Britannica, inc. Accessed August 31, 2022. https://www.britannica.com/place/Jordan/Climate.

67. Williams, Melinda. "Mind Over Matter." Dwell Asia, 2013.
A typical Shop House: Thingsmatter. Accessed August 31, 2022. https://thingsmatter.com/?project=0&dd=0#.

68. "Data.org." Climate. Accessed August 31, 2022. https://en.climate-data.org/asia/thailand/bangkok/bangkok-6313/.

69. Seda, Ediwin. "Al Alfy House / Sha-

hira Fahmy Architects-Archidatum." Archi Datum. Archi Datum, June 7, 2016. http://www.archidatum.com/projects/al-alfy-house-shahira-fahmy-architects/.

70. "Climate: Kuwait." Climate-Data.Org. Climate-Data.Org. Accessed September 4, 2022. https://en.climate-data.org/asia/kuwait-125/.

71. "Hotel Jade." Prendas Loria. Prendas Loria. Accessed September 4, 2022. http://www.prendasloria.com/index.php/hotel-jade/.

72. Climate Data Org. "Data.org." Climate. Climate Data Org. Accessed September 1, 2022. https://en.climate-data.org/north-america/costa-rica-43/.

73. Atelier Vidal. "CASA_MD." Atelier Vidal. Atelier Vidal. Accessed September 1, 2022. https://ateliervidal.com/portfolio/casa_md/.

74. Climate Data Org. "Data.org." Climate. Climate Data Org. Accessed September 1, 2022. https://en.climate-data.org/north-america/jamaica/kingston/kingston-987/.

75. Ishkanes, Jack. "Residential." Jack Ishkanes. Jack Ishkanes. Accessed September 1, 2022. http://jackishkanes.com/work-avenue#/lumen-avenue/. Dar Mabruka: Aga Khan Trust for Culture. "Dar Mabruka Residence-khartoum, Sudan." Archnet. Archnet. Accessed September 1, 2022. https://archnet.org/sites/4523.

76. Climate Data Org. "CLIMATE KHARTOUM." Climate Data Org. Climate Data Org. Accessed September 1, 2022. https://en.climate-data.org/africa/sudan/al-khartum/khartoum-549/.

77. Aguilar, Cristian. "Ebrah Pavillion / Koffi & Diabaté Architectes." ArchDaily. ArchDaily, March 20, 2015. https://www.archdaily.com/607700/ebrah-pavillion-koffi-and-diabate-architectes?ad_source=search&ad_medium=search_result_all.
Ebrah Pavilion: Koffi & Diabaté. "Ebrah Pavilion: Koffi & Diabaté." Koffi & Diabaté | Architects Developers. Koffi & Diabaté, February 9, 2022. https://www.koffi-diabate.com/en/portfolio/pavillon-ebrah/.

78. Climate Data Org. "Climate ASSINIE-MAFIA." Climate Data Org. Climate Data Org. Accessed September 1, 2022. https://en.climate-data.org/africa/cote-d-ivoire/comoe/assinie-mafia-705643/.

79. Form Architects. "Garraway Residence." Form Architects. Form Architects, October 1, 2019. https://www.formarchitects.com/projects-item/garraway-residency/.

80. Climate Data Org. "Climate Jamaica." Climate Data Org. Climate Data Org. Accessed September 1, 2022. https://en.climate-data.org/north-america/jamaica-111/.

81. SDH Studio. "Galipan El Avila by SDH Studio Architecture + Design." SDH_STUDIO Architecture + Design. SDH Studio, July 19, 2022. https://sdhstudio.com/portfolio/el-avila/.

82. Climate Data Org. "CLIMATE CARACAS." Climate Data Org. Climate Data Org. Accessed September 1, 2022. https://en.climate-data.org/south-america/venezuela/distrito-capital/caracas-5677/.

83. Muzia Sforza, Studio Seilern, and Bruce Rowland Architects. "The Gota Dam Residence in Zimbabwe by Sforza Seilern Architects." Livin Spaces. Livin Spaces, January 9, 2022. https://livinspaces.net/design-and-style/livin-homes/gota-dam-residence-zimbabwe-sforza-seilern-architects/.

84. Climate Data Org. "Climate Zimbabwe." Climate Data Org. Climate Data Org. Accessed September 1, 2022. https://en.climate-data.org/africa/zimbabwe-228/.

85. Alarcia ferrer Arquitectos. "JB House: Alarcia-Ferrer Arquitectos." Archello. Archello. Accessed September 1, 2022. https://archello.com/project/jb-house-3.
JB House: Tapia, Daniel. "JB House / Alarciaferrer Arquitectos." ArchDaily. ArchDaily, November 7, 2019. https://www.archdaily.com/927576/jb-house-alarciaferrer-arquitectos.

86. Climate Data Org. "Climate Unquillo." Climate Data Org. Climate Data Org. Accessed September 1, 2022. https://en.climate-data.org/south-america/argentina/cordoba/unquillo-144982.

87. Palinda Kannangara Architects. "Permeable House at Sri Jayawardenapura Kotte." Palinda Kannangara Architects. Palinda Kannangara Architects. Accessed September 1, 2022. https://palindakannangara.com/project/permeable-house-at-sri-jayawardenapura-kotte/.

88. Climate Data Org. "Data Sri Lanka." Climate Data Org. Climate Data Org. Accessed September 1, 2022. https://en.climate-data.org/asia/sri-lanka-256/.

89. Vanuatu Builders. "Master Bungalow-Vanuatu Homes." Vanuatu Builders. Vanuatu Builders. Accessed September 1, 2022. https://vanuatubuilders.vu/portfolio/master-bungalow-2/.

90. "Climate Vanuatu." Climate Data Org. Climate Data Org. Accessed September 1, 2022. https://en.climate-data.org/oceania/vanuatu-109/.

91. José Cubilla & Asociados. "José Cubilla, Federico Cairoli, Vivienda Takuru." Divisare. Divisare. Accessed September 1, 2022. https://divisare.com/projects/395260-jose-cubilla-federico-cairoli-vivienda-takuru.

92. Climate Data Org. "Climate Piribebuy." Climate Data Org. Climate Data Org. Accessed September 1, 2022. https://en.climate-data.org/south-america/paraguay/cordillera/piribebuy-718240/t/february-2/.

93. Caballero, Pilar. "Sencillo Beach House / CmDesign Atelier." ArchDaily. ArchDaily, March 11, 2019. https://www.archdaily.com/912677/sencillo-beach-house-cmdesign-atelier.
Sencillo Beach House: Architecture Art Designs. "Sencillo Beach House Archives." Architecture Art Designs. Architecture Art Designs. Accessed September 1, 2022.
https://www.architectureartdesigns.com/tag/sencillo-beach-house/.

94. Climate Data Org. "Climate Lagos." Climate Data Org. Climate Data Org. Accessed September 1, 2022. https://en.climate-data.org/africa/nigeria/lagos/lagos-552/.

95. Walllasia. "Women's Dormitory & Meditation Building, Wat Pa Wachirabanpot." Walllasia. Accessed September 1, 2022. https://www.walllasia.com/womendormitoryandmeditationbuilding.

96. Climate Data Org. "Climate Chon Buri." Climate Data Org. Climate Data Org. Accessed September 1, 2022. https://en.climate-data.org/asia/thailand/chon-buri-province/chonburi-4203/.

97. MMA Design Studio. "Westwold Way Private Residence." MMA Studio. MMA Design Studio. Accessed September 1, 2022. http://mmastudio.co.za/portfolio/westwold-way-private-residence/.
West World Way Private Residence: Goodwin, Dario. "7 Architects Designing a Diverse Future in Africa." ArchDaily. ArchDaily, February 26, 2015. https://www.archdaily.com/603169/7-architects-designing-a-diverse-future-in-africa

98. Climate Data Org. "Climate Johannesburg." Climate Data Org. Climate Data Org. Accessed September 1, 2022. https://en.climate-data.org/africa/south-africa/gauteng/johannesburg-3221/.

99. NLÉ. NLÉ. Accessed September 1, 2022. http://www.nleworks.com/case/yaba/.

100. Encyclopedia Britannica. "Climate of Nigeria." Encyclopedia Britannica. Encyclopedia Britannica, Inc. Accessed September 1, 2022. https://www.britannica.com/place/Nigeria/Climate.

101. Ramzi, Shanaz. "Retrospective: Yasmeen Lari." Architectural Review, July 21, 2022. https://www.architectural-review.com/buildings/retrospective-yasmeen-lari/10044316.article.

102. "Data.org." Climate. Accessed September 1, 2022. https://en.climate-data.org/asia/pakistan-127/.

103. Admin. "Disaster Relief in Mabwepande." Tawah, January 18, 2016. http://tawahtanzania.or.tz/disaster-relief/.

104. "Tanzania Weather & Climate (+ Climate Chart)." SafariBookings.com. Accessed September 1, 2022. https://www.safaribookings.com/tanzania/climate.

105. Changes in Construction Styles." Guampedia. Accessed September 1, 2022. https://www.guampedia.com/changes-in-construction-styles/. "Kaiser Pre-Fab Homes." Guampedia. Accessed September 1, 2022. https://www.guampedia.com/kaiser-pre-fab-homes/.

106. US Department of Commerce, NOAA. National Weather Service. NOAA's National Weather Service. Accessed September 1, 2022. https://forecast.weather.gov/MapClick.php?lat=13.3873&lon=144.669.

107. "Jintai Village Reconstruction / Rural Urban Framework." ArchDaily. ArchDaily, November 2, 2017. https://www.archdaily.com/882714/jintai-village-reconstruction-rural-urban-framework.

108. "Climate: Sichuan." Climate-Data.Org. Climate-Data.Org. Accessed September 4, 2022. https://en.climate-data.org/asia/china/sichuan-790/.

109. "Her Journey, in Her Own Words LL AR. Brinda Somaya, SNK." YouTube. YouTube, January 14, 2019. https://www.youtube.com/watch?v=AI_qxn-Hfm2o.
Rehabilitation of Bhadli Village: elagoon.com, Glue Lagoon Interactive. "Bhadli Village." Bhadli Village-Bhuj-Architecture. Accessed September 1, 2022. https://www.snkindia.com/project.php?category_id=19&project_id=46.
Rehabilitation of Bhadli Village: Balsavar, Durganand. "Brinda Somaya Says Architects Need to Look beyond the Boundaries of Buildings." Return to frontpage. The Hindu, March 31, 2018. https://www.thehindu.com/society/go-beyond-the-boundaries-of-buildings-60-minutes-with-brinda-somaya/article23398766ece.

110. "Climate: Kutch."Climate-Data.Org. Climate-Data.Org. Accessed September 4, 2022. https://en.climate-data.org/asia/india/kutch-10417/.

111. Pakistan, UNDP. "Green Shelters Inspired by Local Techniques Offer Refuge to Families Affected by the October 2015..." Medium. December 9, 2015. https://medium.com/@UNDP_Pakistan/green-shelters-inspired-by-local-techniques-offer-refuge-to-families-affected-by-the-october-2015-4c3bad662399.

112. "Chitral Climate Info: What's The Weather Like in Chitral, Pakistan." Chitral climate info | What's the weather like in Chitral, Pakistan. Accessed September 1, 2022. https://

www.whatstheweatherlike.org/pakistan/chitral.htm#:~:text=Chitral%20has%20a%20warm%20steppe%20climate%20influenced%20by,longer%20periods%20with%20subzero%20temperatures%20are%20not%20uncommon.

113. "Sangamam." Anupama Kundoo. Accessed September 1, 2022. https://anupamakundoo.com/portfolio-item/sangamam/.
Sangamam Cost-Efficient Habitat: Amy Frearson |7 June 2016 1 comment. "Anupama Kundoo Uses Ferrocement to Create Lego-like House." Dezeen, January 20, 2022. https://www.dezeen.com/2016/06/07/anupama-kundoo-full-fill-homes-ferrocement-house-model-arsenale-venice-architecture-biennale-2016/.

114. "Data.org." Climate. Accessed September 1, 2022. https://en.climate-data.org/asia/india/tamil-nadu/auroville-31587/.

115. "Tunisia: The Troglodyte Dwellings of Matmata." Qantara.de. Accessed September 1, 2022. https://en.qantara.de/content/tunisia-the-troglodyte-dwellings-of-matmata.

116. "Data.org." Climate. Accessed September 1, 2022. https://en.climate-data.org/africa/tunisia-158/.

117. "Cholamandal Center for Contemporary Art." Shilpa Architects. Shilpa Architects Planers Designers, September 10, 2015. http://shilpaarchitects.com/Shilpa_Portfolio/cholamandel-artist-village-museum/.
Cholamandal Artist Village: Cholamandal Artist Village. "Cholamandal (Artist's Village)." Cholamandal (Artist's Village). Accessed August 31, 2022. http://www.cholamandalartistvillage.com/.

118. "Climate and Average Monthly Weather in Mysore (Karnataka), India." World Weather & Climate Information. World Weather & Climate Information. Accessed August 31, 2022. https://weather-and-climate.com/average-monthly-Rainfall-Temperature-Sunshine,mysore,India.

119. NLÉ. "NLÉ." NL. NLÉ. Accessed August 31, 2022. http://www.nleworks.com/case/black-rhino-academy-dormitories/.
Black Rhino Academy: Black Rhino Academy. "The Design of Black Rhino Academy." Black Rhino Academy Foundation. Black Rhino Academy. Accessed August 31, 2022. https://www.blackrhinoacademyfoundation.org/the-design.

120. The World Bank Group. "World Bank Climate Change Knowledge Portal." Climatology | Climate Change Knowledge Portal. The World Bank Group. Accessed August 31, 2022. https://climateknowledgeportal.worldbank.org/country/tanzania/climate-data-historical.

121. MBAD arquitectos. "El Rancho De

Playa Hermosa: Mbad Arquitectos." Archello. Accessed August 31, 2022. https://archello.com/project/el-rancho-de-playa-hermosa.

122. Climate Data Org. "Data.org." Climate. Climate Data Org. Accessed August 31, 2022. https://en.climate-data.org/north-america/united-states-of-america/california/hermosa-beach-16313/.

123. MENÉNDEZ, ANA. "Gando Teachers' Housing by Kéré Architecture." Gando Teachers' Housing by Kéré Architecture | The Strength of Architecture | From 1998. Metalocus. Accessed August 31, 2022. https://www.metalocus.es/en/news/gando-teachers-housing-kere-architecture.
Gando Teacher's Housing: Kéré Architecture. "Kéré: Work." Kéré | Work. Kéré Architecture. Accessed August 31, 2022. https://www.kerearchitecture.com/work/building/gando-teachers-housing.

124. Climatestotravel. "Climate-Burkina Faso https://Www.climatestotravel.com/Climate/Burkina-Faso." Burkina Faso climate: average weather, temperature, precipitation, when to go. Climatestotravel.com. Accessed August 31, 2022. https://www.climatestotravel.com/climate/burkina-faso.

125. Hennigan, Tom. "Marta Moreira." Architectural Record RSS. Architectural Record, November 18, 2015. https://www.architecturalrecord.com/articles/5859-marta-moreira.
Jardim Edite:Hennigan, Tom. "Jardim Edite Social Housing | 2013-03-16 | Architectural Record." Jardim Edite Social Housing. Architectural Record, March 16, 2013. https://www.architecturalrecord.com/articles/7921-jardim-edite-social-housing
Jardim Edite:World Architects. "MMBB Arquitetos-São Paulo, Brazil-Architects-Projects." Brazilian Architects. World Architects. Accessed August 31, 2022. https://www.brazilian-architects.com/en/mmbb-arquitetos-sao-paulo/projects

126. World Weather & Climate Information. "Climate and Average Monthly Weather in Sao Paulo (Sao Paulo State), Brazil." World Weather & Climate Information. Accessed August 31, 2022. https://weather-and-climate.com/average-monthly-Rainfall-Temperature-Sunshine,sao-paulo,Brazil.

127. Gerfen, Katie. "Apan Housing Laboratory, by Mos." Architect Magazine September 4, 2019. https://www.architectmagazine.com/design/apan-housing-laboratory-by-mos_o.
House 8, Apan Housing Laboratory: Brinson, Linda C. "How Adobe Construction Works." HowStuffWorks. April 17, 2012. https://home.howstuffworks.com/home-improvement/construction/materials/adobe-construction.htm.
"House 8, Apan Housing Laboratory." Architect. Architect Magazine, September 4, 2019. https://www.ar-

chitectmagazine.com/project-gallery/house-8-apan-housing-laboratory_o.

128. Weather Spark. "Weatherspark.com." Apan Climate, Weather By Month, Average Temperature (Mexico)-Weather Spark. Weather Spark. Accessed August 31, 2022. https://weatherspark.com/y/6699/Average-Weather-in-Apan-Mexico-Year-Round#:~:text=Average%20Weather%20in%20Apan%20Mexico,or%20above%2081%C2%B0F.

129. Venzon, Marcelo, Julia Park, João Paulo Carrascoza, and Guilherme Pardini. "Ugandan LGBT Youth Asylum Competition Winners Revealed!" Ugandan LGBT Youth Asylum Competition Winners. Beebreeders. Accessed August 31, 2022. https://beebreeders.com/architecturecompetitions/ugandanlgbtyouthasylum/.

130. Climate Data Org. "Data.org." Climate Data. Climate Data Org. Accessed August 31, 2022. https://en.climate-data.org/africa/uganda-160/.

131. NLÉ. "NLÉ." Mabushi Medium Density Residential. NLÉ. Accessed August 31, 2022. http://www.nleworks.com/case/mabushi-medium/.

132. "Climate Change and Conflict in West African Cities: Findings from Lagos, Nigeria and Accra, Ghana." Global Climate Change, January 1, 2013. https://www.climatelinks.org/resources/climate-change-and-conflict-west-african-cities-findings-lagos-nigeria-and-accra-ghana.

133. Orthner, Rosemary, and Martin Orthner. Eco-friendly, affordable housing concept for Ghana. Orthner Orthner & Associates. Accessed August 31, 2022. http://www.orthnerarchitects.com/PROJECTS/Pata4two-2-0/.
Pata4two: Souza, Eduardo. "Colors of the Earth: Ghana's Incredible, Rammed Earth Walls." ArchDaily. November 18, 2021. https://www.archdaily.com/914736/colors-of-the-earth-the-incredible-designs-of-rammed-earth-walls-in-ghana?ad_source=search&ad_medium=search_result_all.

134. Climate Data Org. "Climate-Ghana." Ghana climate: average weather, temperature, precipitation, when to go. Climate Data Org. Accessed August 31, 2022. https://www.climatestotravel.com/climate/ghana.

135. MASS Design Group. "Masaka Affordable Housing." MASS Design Group. MASS Design Group. Accessed August 31, 2022. https://massdesigngroup.org/work/design/masaka-affordable-housing.
Masaka Affordable Housing: Frearson, Amy. "10 African Architects and Designers Championing Afrofuturism." Dezeen. April 6, 2018. https://www.dezeen.com/2018/04/06/african-architects-designers-championing-afrofuturism/.

136. Climate Data Org. "Data.org." Climate. Cilmate Data Org. Accessed August 31, 2022. https://en.climate-data.org/africa/rwanda/kigali-city/kigali-1044/.

137. Franco, José Tomás. "Prototype Housing I / Collective Studio." ArchDaily. May 21, 2013. https://www.archdaily.com/374175/prototype-housing-i-collective-studio. Collective Studio is an architectural practice based in Phnom Penh, Divisare. "Divisare." Collective Studio · Divisare. Accessed August 31, 2022. https://divisare.com/authors/2144720704-collective-studio.

138. Climate Data Org. "Data.org." Climate. Climate Data Org. Accessed August 31, 2022. https://en.climate-data.org/asia/cambodia-167/.

139. Busta, Hallie. "Quinta Monroy Housing." Architect. Elemental, January 13, 2016. https://www.architectmagazine.com/project-gallery/quinta-monroy-housing_o. Quinta Monroy Housing: Tory-Henderson, Nina. "Quinta Monroy." DAC. Architect Magazine, August 31, 2022. https://dac.dk/en/knowledgebase/architecture/quinta-monroy.

140. Climate Data Org. "Data.org." Climate. Climate Data Org. Accessed August 31, 2022. https://en.climate-data.org/south-america/chile/i-region-de-tarapaca/iquique-2051/.

141. CM Design Atelier. "The Plum Apartments." CMD+A. CM Design Atelier. Accessed August 31, 2022. https://www.cmdesign-atelier.com/portfolios/the-plum-apartments/.

142. World Weather & Climate Information. "Climate and Average Monthly Weather in Lagos, Nigeria." World Weather & Climate Information. Accessed August 31, 2022. https://weather-and-climate.com/average-monthly-Rainfall-Temperature-Sunshine,lagos-ng,Nigeri.

143. Kéré Architecture. "Home." Kéré. Kéré Architecture. Accessed August 31, 2022. https://www.kerearchitecture.com/. Songtaaba Women's Center: Goodwin, Dario. "7 Architects Designing a Diverse Future in Africa." ArchDaily. February 26, 2015. https://www.archdaily.com/603169/7-architects-designing-a-diverse-future-in-africa.

144. Climate Data Org. "Data.org." Climate. Climate Data Org. Accessed August 31, 2022. https://en.climate-data.org/africa/burkina-faso-14/.

145. Gaete, Javier. "Villa for Girls / Soliscolomer y Asociados." ArchDaily. October 28, 2013. https://www.archdaily.com/441922/villa-for-girls-soliscolomer-y-asociados?ad_medium=office_landing&ad_name=article.

146. Climate Data Org. "Data.org." Climate. Climate Data Org. Accessed August 31, 2022. https://

en.climate-data.org/north-america/honduras/francisco-morazan/tegucigalpa-3766/#:~:text=The%20Tegucigalpa%20lies%20on%20933m,Tegucigalpa%20has%20a%20tropical%20climate.&text=The%20climate%20here%20is%20classified,is%201002%20mm%20%7C%2039.4%20inch.

147. World Habitat. "Viviendas Del Hogar De Cristo, Guayaquil." World Habitat, March 27, 2018. https://world-habitat.org/world-habitat-awards/winners-and-finalists/viviendas-del-hogar-de-cristo-guayaquil/#award-content.
The Viviendas del Hogar de Cristo: Londoño, Ximena. "News & Events: Jorge Moran Ubidia, Ecuador." World Bamboo Organization. Accessed August 31, 2022. https://worldbamboo.net/news-and-events/bamboo-pioneers/jorge-moran-ubidia-ecuador

148. Climate Data Org. "Data.org." Climate. Climate Data Org. Accessed August 31, 2022. https://en.climate-data.org/south-america/ecuador/provincia-del-guayas/guayaquil-2962/.

149. Henry, Elizabeth G., Katherine Semrau, Davidson H. Hamer, Taryn Vian, Mary Nambao, Kaluba Mataka, and Nancy A. Scott. "The Influence of Quality Maternity Waiting Homes on Utilization of Facilities for Delivery in Rural Zambia." Reproductive Health 14, no. 1 (2017). https://doi.org/10.1186/s12978-017-0328-z.
Woldyia Maternity Center: Singhal, Sumit. "Woldyia Maternity Center in Ethiopia by Vilalta Arquitectura." ArchShowcase. September 8, 2017. https://www10.aeccafe.com/blogs/arch-showcase/2017/09/08/woldyia-maternity-center-in-ethiopia-by-vilalta-arquitectura/.
Flinstone, Vilalta Studio. "Tsedeke Yihunie Woldu." Vilalta Studio. Vilalta Studio. Accessed August 31, 2022. https://vilalta.studio/en/#profile

150. Climatestotravel. "Climate-Ethiopia." Ethiopia climate: average weather, temperature, precipitation, when to go. Climatestotravel. Accessed August 31, 2022. https://www.climatestotravel.com/climate/ethiopia.

Architects Directory

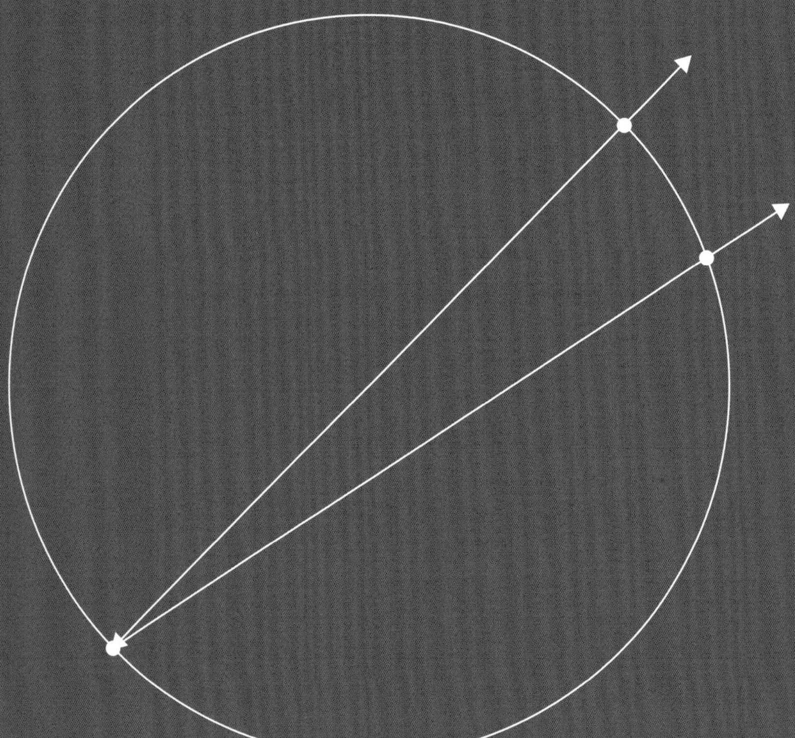

R/N	Architect/Firm	Birth year	Country	University
-	Cristián Olivi and Diego Ortúzar 2172 / Asociados	-	Chile	- -
65A	Joaquín Pérez Goicoechea and Nasser B. Abulhasan AGi Architects	-	Kuwait	Harvard United States
65B	Alarcia Ferrer Arquitectos	-	Argentina	Catholic University of Cordoba Spain
65C	Almimariya Architects and Designers for Sustainable Development	-	Lebanon	M.I.T United States
65D	Ana Rascovsky Ana Rascovsky Arqs	1972	Argentina	Berlage Institute, Rotterdam Netherlands
65E	Anupama Kundoo Anupama Kundoo Architects	1967	India	University of Madrid Spain
-	Irene Joselevich ARQA	-	Argentina	- -
65F	Mariam Kamara Atelier Masomi	-	Niger	University of Washington United States
- -	Ayeneh Office	-	Iran	- -
-	Badri Qadah Badri Qadah	-	Iran	- -
-	Enrico Chinellato, and Jacopo Donato Bee Breeders, Enrico Chinellato, Jacopo Donato	-	Uganda	- -
66A	Bilal Hammad	-	Jordan	University of Alexandria Egypt
66B	Budi Pradono	-	Indonesia	Berlage Institute, Rotterdam Netherlands

R/N	Architect/Firm	Birth year	Country	University
168I	Johann Slee Slee & co Architects	-	Namibia	University of KwaZulu-Natal South Africa
168J	Mauricio Solís Solis Colomer y Associados	-	Honduras	Universidad Francisco Marroquin Guatemala
168K	Brinda Somaya Somaya and Kalappa Consultants	1940	India	Mumbai University India
-	Mariano Donoso Rea Sommet & Asociados	-	Bolivia	- -
169A	Benjamin Garcia Saxe Studio Saxe	-	Costa Rica	Rhode Island School of Design United States
169B	Mauricio Rocha, Gabriela Carillo Taller Mauricio Rocha & Gabriela Carillo	1965, 1987	Mexico	National Autonomous School of Mexico Mexico
-		-	Tanzania	- -
-	Urko Sánchez Urko Sangchez Architects	-	Dijibouti	- -
-	Vanatu Builders	-	Vanatu	- -
169C	Julio Vilamajó Vilamajó, Pucciarelli & Carve Company	-	Uruguay	Faculty of Architecture and MNAV -
169D	Vo Trong Nghia Vo Trong Nghia Architects	-	Vietnam	University of Tokyo Japan
169E	BC Ang and Wen Hsia Ang WHBC Architects	-	Malaysia	Universiti Teknologi Malaysia Malaysia
-	Rula Yaghmour Yaghmour Architects	-	Jordan	- -
169F	Yasmeen Lari Yasmeen Lari	1941	Pakistan	Oxford School of Architecture England

SOFIE KUSABA
B.ARCH' 21
Editor, Writer

Sofie Kusaba is a multidisciplinary musician, architect, writer, and digital artist who is currently interested in the intersection of queer identity, intergernational and interdependent communities through both physical and digital atmospheres. Sofie is a recent graduate from the Rhode Island School of Design with a Bachelor's degree in Architecture and Fine Arts. In her final degree project, she remodeled the danchi, a post WWII nuclear family housing typology, into an accountability living support network between an intergenerational community. She worked on a zine that focused on alternative sharing and support structures through an adaptive reuse framework, and was featured at the Tokyo Art Book Fair, at the Museum of Contemporary Art in Tokyo. Currently she is working for the New York based firm, HWKN, on Canada Water, a coworking resort space for remote tech workers in London. She also co-operates a bespoke fantasy jewelry business with Alison Sherpa called PEMA KO. Prior to working at HWKN, she was an intern at Junya Ishigami + Associates and worked on the Tokushima Arts and Culture Hall competition that became the winning entry.

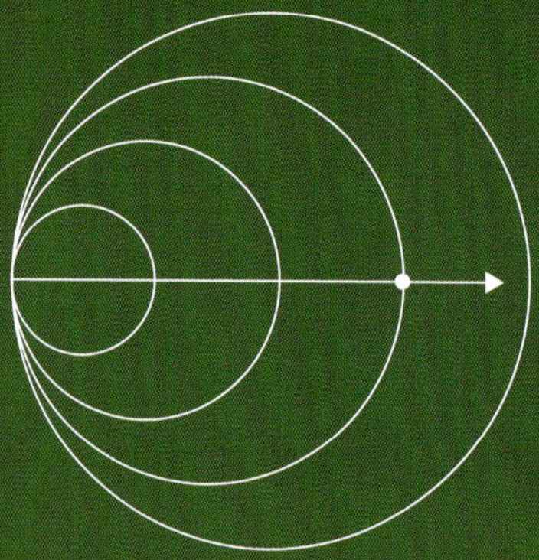

HRISTINA TRUWIT
1. ARCH' 21
ditor, Writer

hristina Truwit (she/her) is a Provi- ence-based architectural researcher, esigner and artist. She received her 1Arch degree from RISD after attending llegheny College for her degree in Math- matics and Studio Art. Her work studies he intersection of sustainability, social ıstice and uncovering hidden narratives. he won an award for her thesis project roperties, Borders and Sites: An Order f Operations, in which she investigated ow the arrangement of the built environ- nent interacts with climate change. Her vork was showcased at the RISD Muse- m and at the WaterFire Arts Center.

ruwit teaches in the Architecture epartment at RISD, and is a founder nd coordinator of Project Archive, a rant-run research collective aimed at ecentralizing the research process and xpanding the Western canon. She spoke t the Association of Collegiate Schools f Architecture National Conference and he Association of Architecture School f Librarians National Conference about onstructing digital archives and the dan- er of a single story. She has also worked n community-led housing projects for eople experiencing homelessness in 1inneapolis, and as a sustainable ar- hitectural designer for Prendas Loria ocated in Nosara, Costa Rica.

NAMRATA DHORE
B.ARCH' 21
Founder, Editor, Writer

Namrata Dhore is a designer and researcher based in New York. She is currently pursuing her M.S. in Advanced Architectural Design at Columbia University. She has previously attended Rhode Island School of Design and received a BFA and Bachelor's in Architecture. She also received the Warren Family Award upon Graduation and honors for her work for Project Archive. She has also worked on projects for the RISD Museum in Providence and A.I.R. Gallery in New York. She has also presented her work at the ACSA 2021 and AASL 2022 conferences along with her colleagues Sofie Kusaba and Christina Truwit. She continues to shape her practice to accommodate environmentally resilient architectural design and development in urban spaces.

Colophon

Published by Applied Research and Design Publishing, an imprint of ORO Editions.
Gordon Goff: Publisher

www.appliedresearchanddesign.com
info@appliedresearchanddesign.com

AUTHORS:-
INTRODUCTION:-
BOOK DESIGN: ILVZ STUDIO
EDITOR: NAMRATA DHORE, SOFIE KUSABA & CHRISTINA TRUWIT
PROJECT MANAGER: JAKE ANDERSON

10 9 8 7 6 5 4 3 2 1 First Edition

ISBN: 978-1-957183-47-3

Color Separations and Printing: ORO Group Inc.
Printed in China.

AR+D Publishing makes a continuous effort to minimize the overall carbon footprint of its publications. As part of this goal, AR+D, in association with Global ReLeaf, arranges to plant trees to replace those used in the manufacturing of the paper produced for its books. Global ReLeaf is an international campaign run by American Forests, one of the world's oldest nonprofit conservation organizations. Global ReLeaf is American Forests' education and action program that helps individuals, organizations, agencies, and corporations improve the local and global environment by planting and caring for trees.